This book belongs to ....

To the people of Bylakuppe who shared their stories with me and welcomed me into their homes and hearts.

— Aaniya Asrani

Special thanks to:
Srishti School of Art, Design and Technology, especially Dr Geetha Narayanan, Meera Curam, Kavita Arvind and Srivi Kalyan, for their kind support in the making of this book.

HOMECOMING

Aaniya Asrani

KATHA

This book is a part of a series of creative non-fiction books based on the lives of Tibetan refugees living in Bylakuppe, Karnataka, India.

The Tibetan people sought refuge in India in 1959 when their country fell into the hands of the People's Republic of China. 150,000 Tibetans followed their spiritual and political leader Tenzin Gyatso, the 14th Dalai Lama, and started living in settlements across India.

This is the story of one such Tibetan refugee ...

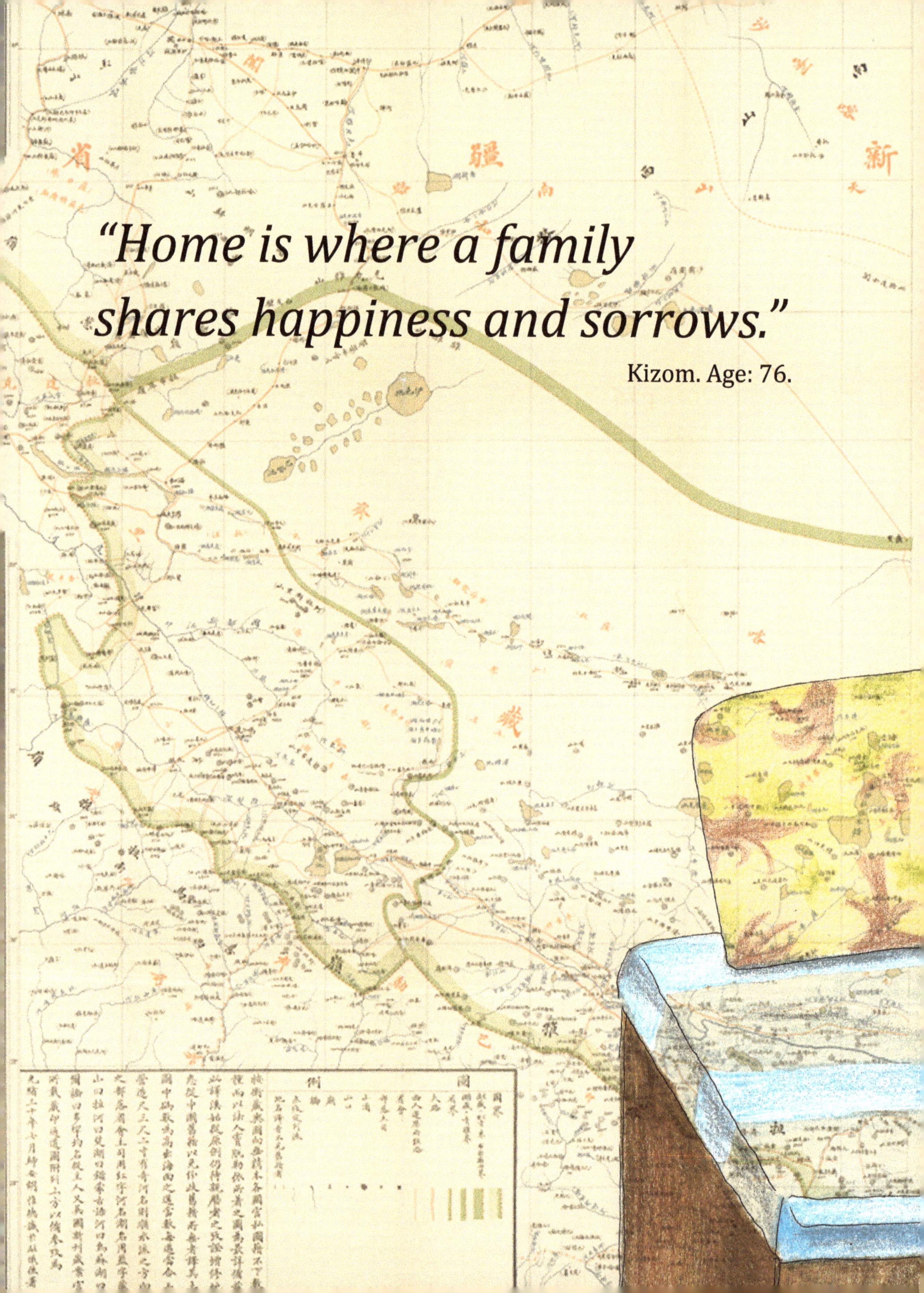
“Home is where a family shares happiness and sorrows.”
Kizom. Age: 76.

PORT

I was born into a family of nomadic cattle-herders in Tibet. We moved around the plateaus — going to the higher altitudes in summers and coming down to the foothills in winters.

We lived in a big tent made of woven yak hair. It protected us from the harsh weather.

Nomadic [noh-mad-ik]: living by travelling from place to place

Altitude [al-ti-tude]: height above sea level

We had many cattle to take care of.

I remember once my parents decided to let my cousin and me graze the yaks in the field while they did the other chores.

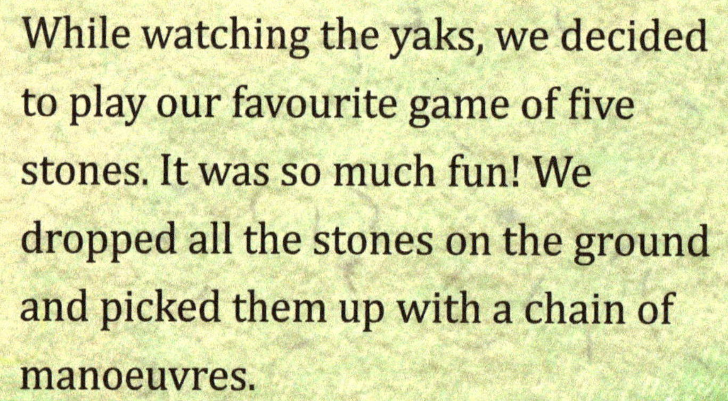

While watching the yaks, we decided to play our favourite game of five stones. It was so much fun! We dropped all the stones on the ground and picked them up with a chain of manoeuvres.

Manoeuvre [muh-noo-ver]: a series of moves

We were so engrossed in the game that we didn't notice that the yaks had wandered away in every direction.

Engross [en-grohs]: to be occupied completely

Imagine our surprise when the game was finally over and all the yaks had disappeared!

We managed to find three of them, but still got an earful from our parents.

Earful [eer-full]: scolding

Polur
UNEXPLO

When I was nineteen, I met my friend Choden one day. She told me that the Chinese were coming to force us to recite poems against the Dalai Lama.

She also told me that she was running away to India.

I too didn't want to live in a Tibet that was turning against the Dalai Lama.

I made the decision to run away with her.

I left without telling my parents. They must have assumed that I had been taken away by Yama, the God of Death.

UNEXPLOR
LHASA
Zhikatse

When I first arrived in Bylakuppe, I helped in clearing the forest area that was allotted to Tibetan refugees by the Indian Government. I also helped in the construction of the Tibetan Children's Village where young children still come to study.

Now I am old and live in an old age home in Bylakuppe. I had left Tibet in a hurry. All I carried in the folds of my *chuba* were the stones we used to play with, and the Indian coins we wore as trinkets in our hair.

Some school children come to visit me on Sundays. They bring me gifts that I add to my collection!

Chuba [chu-ba]: a Tibetan costume

On Losar, the children brought me a scarf.

Sometimes I close my eyes and imagine my younger self dancing with the scarf around my neck!

Losar [lo-sar]: the Tibetan New Year

But I have nothing to remind me of my family in Tibet, and I have no way to contact them.

Even though I am happy in the old age home,
I wish I could meet my family again.

I am too old now to think of another home.
This old age home is my final resting place.

But I will continue to dream about a
reunited family in Tibet.

What does 'home' mean to you?

Use this space to share stories of your home with Kizom!

Aaniya Asrani is a mixed-media illustrator, graphic designer and traveller from Bangalore, India. She is interested in telling diverse and unheard stories, and aims to start a conversation about human condition and identity, in order to sensitise future generations about the adverse effects of large social and political movements.

KATHA

Katha is a globally recognised non-profit organization (www.katha.org) that has been working in the literacy to literature continuum since 1988. Our nearly 30 years of experience is in publishing and education for children in poverty.

"An educational jewel in India's crown." **— Naoyuki Shinohara, Deputy Managing Director, IMF**

"Katha stands as an exemplar for all the creative projects around the world that grapple with ordinary and dramatic misery in cities." **— Charles Landry, *The Art of City Making***

"Katha has a real soft corner for kids. Which is why it ... create[s] such gorgeous picture books for children." **— Time Out**

"Katha's work is driven by the idea that children can bring change to their communities that is sustainable and real, just as the children do in [their books.]" **— Papertigers**

First published by Katha, 2018

ISBN 978-93-88284-05-9

Our Mission: Every child reading well and for fun!

I Love Reading Library is a unique series of books that brings new/ diffident readers into sustainable learning. With high-quality content and design to match the learning needs of children at different reading levels, it brings the best of India's 2000 years of literary heritage. Based on StoryPedagogy devised by Geeta Dharmarajan, these books help increase young readers' ability to understand BIG ideas for change and help them build a kinder, more sustainable world.

A3, Sarvodaya Enclave, Sri Aurobindo Marg, New Delhi 110 017

Phone: 4141 6600 . 4182 9998 . 2652 1752 . Fax: 2651 4373

E-mail: marketing@katha.org, Website: www.katha.org

Ten per cent of sales proceeds from this book will support the quality education of children studying in Katha Schools.

Katha regularly plants trees to replace the wood used in the making of its books.

home away from home!

India is home to several Tibetans living in exile. They live in close-knitted clusters across India, and form a vibrant and peaceful community. Some of the main Tibetan settlements in India are in Dharamshala and McLeod Ganj in Himachal Pradesh, Bylakuppe in Karnataka, and Darjeeling in West Bengal.

The Tibetans brought with them stories and colours from their homeland. They work closely with the handicraft sector of India and create beautiful artworks in stone, wood and textiles. Through this, they are able to preserve the spirit of Tibet while making us culturally richer and more vibrant!

www.ingramcontent.com/pod-product-compliance
Ingram Content Group UK Ltd.
Pitfield, Milton Keynes, MK11 3LW, UK
UKHW062005290726
14090UKWH00022B/1404